# Taking Leave of Your Home

# Taking Leave of Your Home

*Moving in the Peace of Christ*

Mark G. Boyer

WIPF & STOCK · Eugene, Oregon

TAKING LEAVE OF YOUR HOME
Moving in the Peace of Christ

Wipf & Stock
An Imprint of Wipf and Stock Publishers
199 W. 8th Ave., Suite 3
Eugene, OR 97401

www.wipfandstock.com

PAPERBACK ISBN: 978-1-4982-9799-8
HARDCOVER ISBN: 978-1-4982-9801-8
EBOOK ISBN: 978-1-4982-9800-1

Manufactured in the U.S.A.                                        JULY 5, 2016

Dedicated to the Members of my LIMEX Group

1997—2000

William Bishop

Melissa Bosso

Nancy Derryberry

Joan Keiser

Cyndi (Love) Berry

Clarence McKay

Rebecca Pruitt

Lucy Synk

# Contents

# Introduction

We are pilgrims on a journey. And for many of us that means we will leave our home and move to another one at least once during our lifetime pilgrimage. While we have many rituals for entering and blessing a new home, we have little or nothing for taking leave of the place we have called home for years or months. This book is a resource for taking leave of a home, no matter if it has to be done quickly, is caused by some kind of disaster, or can be done slowly over a period of weeks.

Taking leave of a home resembles taking leave of a deceased family member or friend. Elisabeth Kubler-Ross has identified five stages that people pass through in taking leave of their lives: denial, anger, bargaining, depression, and acceptance. Later, she concluded that the living pass through the same stages in taking leave of the deceased. Likewise, when moving from one home to another, family members pass through the same stages.

First, they deny that the move will have to be made. Then, they get angry at having to sort through and box up everything in preparation for the move. Bargaining enters in when some family members want to stay behind and finish a school year, complete a project, or see an activity to its conclusion. Depression enters in as family members face the physical, psychological, social, and spiritual work of taking leave of their home. Finally, all accept that they will have to move and that there is nothing to do but enter into the process.

# Introduction

Charles Corr, Clyde Nabe, and Donna Corr offer a task-based approach for coping with dying which can easily be applied to leaving one's home and moving to another. They isolate four primary areas of task work that must be done based on the four dimensions of the life of a human being: the physical, the psychological, the social, and the spiritual.

Applying their task-based approach to moving, we see that the physical tasks of leave-taking include sorting through everything a family owns, boxing everything, and maybe in this day of rent-a-moving-van even physically carrying every boxed item and piece of furniture out of the old home and into the new one. The psychological task involves leaving the security, the familiarity, and the emotions attached to one's home and embracing the insecurity, the unfamiliarity, and the lack of any emotional attachment yet to the new home. Leaving behind friends and family and a church community and other groups to which family members belong comprises the work of the social task, which will not be completed until the move is finished and memberships in new communities are established. The work of the spiritual task, which is not the same as church or religion, consists of establishing the new home as a place of meaning for the family, a place where members are connected to each other, and a place of transcendence where people find hope and are able to make contributions to the world. While not demeaning the importance of the other tasks, this book focuses primarily on the psychological and spiritual tasks of taking leave of one's home.

Chapter 1 offers suggestions on how to take leave of one's home slowly. It enables a family to embrace some of both the psychological and the spiritual tasks of leaving-taking. A few weeks before a family has to leave its home members begin to gather every day or every other day in a different room to pray, to share memories, and to take leave of that room.

Chapter 2 presents occasions when one must quickly take leave of a home because of poor health, a health emergency, age, the death of a spouse, finances, a job transfer, etc. When one must leave his or her home quickly and there is no time to take leave over several weeks or even several days, it is important to face the move with as many members of one's family as possible. Even if one has to mark the leave-taking alone, it is important to acknowledge that for whatever reasons one is moving and prayer helps to facilitate the transition.

Because nature can precipitate a move, chapter 3 offers suggestions for taking leave of a home when one has been faced with such a disaster as a tornado, a flood, an earthquake, a fire, etc. Leaving a home after it has been destroyed in a disaster assists in the psychological task. With as many members of the family as possible a family gathers near the place where the home stood or on the site where it was built, and they acknowledge that they must move. After a few moments of prayer, they take leave of their home.

Chapter 4 presents a short prayer service to be held on moving day. The final prayer said on moving day should be conducted in the home. After gathering the members of the family and any who are assisting in the move into one of the empty rooms of the home, the family members ritually take leave of their home and begin their journey to their new home.

This book is designed to be used by families for prayer. A five-part exercise is offered for every one of the entries.

1. In chapter 1 the names of the rooms in the home form the sub-headlines and indicate where the members of the family should gather. In chapters 2 and 3 the reasons for leaving one's home are the sub-headlines.

2. Each section of every chapter presents a few verses of a biblical or Scripture text that is appropriate for the topic under consideration.

3. A reflection follows. The reflection is based on the biblical text in the context of taking leave of one's home. An individual may read the reflection, or one person of a family may read it aloud for others.

   Throughout the reflections I use the masculine pronoun for God, LORD, LORD God, etc. I am well aware that God is neither male nor female, but in order to avoid the repetition of nouns over and over again, I employ male pronouns, as they are also used throughout most biblical translations.

4. The reflection is followed by an activity which involves the members of a family in some way. Most of the time, the activity invites family members to share an experience with one another. The activity functions as a guide for personal appropriation of the message of the reflection. After a few minutes of sharing, family members are ready to conclude the exercise.

5. A prayer concludes the exercise and summarizes the theme explored in the reflection which served as the foundation for the activity. One member of a family may say the prayer for all, or all may proclaim the prayer together.

In no moving experience will all the entries presented here be used. This book is designed to function as a resource for families, who, for whatever reason, find that they need to move. For example, not every home has all the rooms listed in chapter 1. Therefore, only what is needed should be chosen from the possibilities presented.

Furthermore, since it is not possible to foresee every possible occasion when people may be taking leave of a home, the reader/user of this book should choose what he or she needs from the resources provided. It is the author's prayer that he or she will be able to take leave of his or her home in the peace of Christ.

Mark G. Boyer

*chapter one*

# Slowly Taking Leave of One's Home

For most people a move from one home to another is a planned event. The family members have plenty of time to take leave of their home slowly. A few weeks before you have to leave your home, take a few minutes every day or every other day to gather the members of your family into a different room as specified below and, after prayer, take leave of that room. Choose a time, like morning or evening that will facilitate the presence of all family members.

# The Family Room

**Scripture:** ". . . I bow my knees before the Father, from whom every family in heaven and on earth takes its name. I pray that, according to the riches of his glory, he may grant that you may be strengthened in your inner being with power through his Spirit, and that Christ may dwell in your hearts through faith, as you are being rooted and grounded in love." (Eph 3:14–17)

**Reflection:** The family room is one of the most important rooms in any home. Here the family gathers to watch TV, to play video and board games, to read the paper, to talk, to finish homework, and much more. A family is most itself in the family room. God first brought together the man and woman who became husband and wife. Then, God brought forth from their union the children who help populate the family room.

It is from God, then, that every family comes. The spirit of each family member mingles with the spirit of every other family member—that's how God shares the Holy Spirit. The Christ who dwells in each family member strengthens the Christ in every other family member through his or her love for all others.

Of course, father, mother, and children form only one kind of family. There are also single-parent families, foster families, blended families, and other kinds of families. It's not the type of family that is important in taking leave of the family room; it's the rootedness and groundedness in love that has occurred through every family member that is remembered in the family room.

**Activity:** Ask each member of the family to sit in a circle on the floor of the family room and share an experience of feeling loved there. After all have shared say the following prayer.

**Prayer:** God of love, in this room your have strengthened us with your Spirit of love and formed us into your family. We acknowledge that all the love we have shown each other comes from you. Help us to take the love we have shared in this room to our family room in our new house. Continue to strengthen us with your love as we continue to strengthen each other by sharing your love with each other. We ask this through Jesus Christ our Lord. Amen.

**Leader**: Let us take leave of this family room in the peace of Christ.

**All**: Thanks be to God.

# The Dining Room

**Scripture**: ". . . Jacob made a vow, saying, 'If God will be with me, and will keep me in this way that I go, and will give me bread to eat and clothing to wear, so that I come again to my father's house in peace, then the LORD shall be my God, and this stone, which I have set up for a pillar, shall be God's house; and of all that you give me I will surely give one tenth to you.'" (Gen 28:20–22)

**Reflection**: No matter if the dining room is used on a regular basis or only for special occasions, it may be the most important room in the house. At its center is a table with enough chairs for every member of the family to gather around it. The life of the family flows from the dining room because that is where food is placed for everyone to eat. In other words, the life of the family is sustained by the food on the dining room table.

However, when people pass around bowls of food, they also pass around themselves. When they pass the mashed potatoes, they also pass some of who each person is. Listen to the level of conversation around the dining room table. Everyone wants to talk at once; everyone wants to share some of who he or she is. When all have eaten their fill of the food, all are also full of the other members of the family.

The patriarch Jacob recognized that everything, but especially food, was a gift from God. He promised to return to God one tenth of everything that God entrusted to Jacob's care. And that's exactly what a family does around the dining room table. Each member gives of himself or herself to all others because each has received an abundance from God.

**Activity**: As all family members are seated around the dining room table, turn down or turn off the lights, light a candle and place it in the middle of the table, and ask each person to share some special occasion, event, discussion, or announcement of an event that took place in the dining room. When the sharing is finished, say the prayer below and extinguish the candle.

**Prayer**: God who gives us every gift, hear our prayer of thanksgiving for all that we have shared around this table—for the special occasions of birthday meals and funeral meals, for our lively discussions, for the announcements that we have made. As we take leave of this dining room, help us to take with us all that we have shared with each other, and enable us to continue to share all that you have given us through Jesus Christ our Lord. Amen.

**Leader**: Let us take leave of this dining room in the peace of Christ.

**All**: Thanks be to God.

# The Kitchen

**Scripture**: "When Isaac was old and his eyes were dim so that he could not see, he called his elder son Esau and said to him . . . , 'See I am old; I do not know the day of my death. Now then, take your weapons, your quiver and your bow, and go out to the field and hunt game for me. Then prepare for me savory food, such as I like, and bring it to me to eat, so that I may bless you before I die.'" (Gen 27:1–4)

**Reflection**: While the patriarch Esau, Jacob's brother, had to prepare the game he hunted and killed for his father over a camp fire, he would have probably preferred a kitchen with today's display of appliances and pantry supplied with food. Instead of watching and turning the roasting game on a spit, he could have time-baked it in an electric oven with a motorized spit. Instead of boiling vegetables in a pot over the open flame, he could have put them in a microwave oven in a serving bowl. He wouldn't have had to walk to the river to get water; he could have turned on the faucet and gotten hot, cold, or any range of temperatures in between.

In the kitchen of our home food has been prepared for many different occasions. Ordinary meals have been baked with care. Snacks have been warmed. Thanksgiving turkeys, Christmas geese, and Easter hams with all the trimmings have occupied much of people's time in the kitchen. Maybe even some meals, such as breakfast, have been eaten in a nook or around a counter in the kitchen.

The kitchen, then, is the source of our sustenance as a family. The food that we need to stay alive first arrives in our home in the kitchen, where it is stored and made ready for human consumption. So, as one takes leave of a home, it is important to remember the storehouse of energy that the kitchen has been for the family.

**Activity**: Gather all family members in the kitchen and ask each one to share what place (cabinet, refrigerator, freezer, breakfast nook, etc.) or event (baking cookies, cooking a meal, roasting a turkey, etc.) is of the most importance to him or her in the kitchen and why. After all have shared say the following prayer.

**Prayer**: Eternal Source of Life, we acknowledge that all sustenance comes from you. So, we give you thanks for all the food that we have shared from this kitchen, for all the events that have taken place in it, and for your blessings that have been received here. May we take with us the memories of the meals we have received here to our new home where we trust that you will continue to nourish us through Jesus Christ our Lord. Amen.

**Leader**: Let us take leave of this kitchen in the peace of Christ.

**All**: Thanks be to God.

# The Living Room

**Scripture**: ". . . Gideon went into his house and prepared a kid, and unleavened cakes from an ephah of flour; the meat he put in a basket, and the broth he put in a pot, and brought them to [the angel of the LORD] under the oak and presented them. The angel of God said to him, 'Take the meat and the unleavened cakes, and put them on this rock, and pour out the broth.' And he did so. Then the angel of the LORD reached out the tip of the staff that was in his hand, and touched the meat and the unleavened cakes; and fire sprang up from the rock and consumed the meat and the unleavened cakes; and the angel of the LORD vanished from his sight." (Judg 6:18–21)

**Reflection**: In many living rooms the center of attention is the fireplace. In ancient days, the fireplace was important because its burning wood gave off heat and light. At the fireplace meats were roasted, water was boiled, and stews were simmered. Today, few people even burn wood in their fireplaces; most are now equipped with gas logs.

But there is nothing more warming that a fireplace. People gather around it to talk, to eat a snack, to pray, to play. The fireplace in the living room may be the gathering spot for one's family on a cold winter's night. Or someone may curl up on a chair or sofa next to it with a good book for an evening of reading.

Since the invention of fire, people have gathered around a fire ring, a camp fire, a stove, a fireplace. Fire draws us to its source. That's why fire is used throughout the Bible as a sign of God's presence. Moses experienced God through a burning bush. Isaiah discovered God in the fire and smoke in the temple in Jerusalem. And Gideon witnessed God consuming his offering with fire in the person of the angel of the LORD. God draws people together with fire.

**Activity**: Light a fire in your fireplace. Gather all the family members together and ask each of them to share a memory of an event that took place in the living room. When all are finished, either turn off the gas logs or let the fire die and sit in silence for a while. Then, say the prayer below.

**Prayer**: God of fire, you have revealed yourself to us in this living room just as you disclosed your presence in fire to Moses, Isaiah, and Gideon. Help us to carry the fire of your presence to our new home where you will come and live with us. We give you thanks for all the special moments that we have shared in this living room through Jesus Christ our Lord. Amen.

**Leader**: Let us take leave of this living room in the peace of Christ.

**All**: Thanks be to God.

# The Master Bedroom

**Scripture**: "Let mutual love continue. Let marriage be held in honor by all, and let the marriage bed be kept undefiled . . . ." (Heb 13:1, 4)

**Reflection**: The room in which adult family leaders sleep is often referred to as the master bedroom; in many homes it is the largest bedroom in the house and features a private bathroom.
It is considered to be the private place of those who lead and guide the family.

In the ancient world the room housing the marriage bed was of utmost importance because it was the place where marriage was consummated, love was made, and children were conceived. The master bedroom occupied a place of honor in the home.

Today, the master bedroom is the private place for the adult leaders of a family. Adults can enjoy the privacy of the bedroom to discuss important issues. They nourish their unique relationship in the bedroom, where they consummate their relationship by making love. And if they are given to them, they conceive children in that room. So, the master bedroom is an appropriate place from which the members of a family, especially its leaders, take leave.

**Activity**: Adult family leaders may choose to either gather the other members of the family in their bedroom or to engage in this activity alone. They share what they consider the most important event to have taken place in the master bedroom. Then, they say the following prayer.

**Prayer**: God of love, you nourish our relationship with you through your gift of grace which we, in turn, share with each other. We know that you have blessed us in this bedroom, that you have shared your love with us, as we have shared it with each other, and that from here we have shared it with the other members of our family. Grant that we may take this love with us to our new home that it may make our bedroom holy through Jesus Christ our Lord. Amen.

**Leader**: Let us take leave of this master bedroom in the peace of Christ.

**All**: Thanks be to God.

# The Child(ren)'s Bedroom(s)

**Scripture**: ". . . We were gentle among you, like a nurse tenderly caring for her own children. So deeply do we care for you that we are determined to share with you not only the gospel of God but also our own selves, because you have become very dear to us." (1 Thess 2:7–8)

**Reflection**: The child's or children's bedroom is the first place that a child calls "my room." Not only does he or she sleep in that room, but he or she also often prays and plays and may even bathe in that room. The room may have been called a nursery, but as the child grows it quickly becomes identified with the person who sleeps in the bed there. Parents share their lives with their children in their bedroom, where they console them, bless them, and take care of their myriad of needs. For the teenager, the child's or children's room is the person's private space.

Not only is moving difficult for children because they have to start over making friends and getting used to a new house and neighborhood and school, but it is hard because one's childhood is being left behind. The room in which one grew up is being vacated and that forces the child or young person further into the adult world.

So, it is very appropriate for children to take leave of their room. In doing so they are taking leave of a part of their lives and preparing to embrace the next step of their journey.

**Activity**: Gather all her members of the family in the child's or children's bedroom and ask each child to share what he or she considers to be the most important event to have taken place in his or her bedroom. Then, say the following prayer.

**Prayer**: God our Father and Mother, you bring us to birth, sustain us on our lifetime journey, and bring us home to you. As we prepare to take leave of this bedroom, may we remember the growth that has taken place in the person who lived here and how he or she has nourished the growth of the other members of our family. Help all of us to continue to grow in your grace in our new home through Jesus Christ our Lord. Amen.

**Leader**: Let us take leave of this bedroom in the peace of Christ.

**All**: Thanks be to God.

# The Guest Room

**Scripture**: "One day Elisha was passing through Shunem, where a wealthy woman lived, who urged him to have a meal. So whenever he passed that way, he would stop there for a meal. She said to her husband, 'Look, I am sure that this man who regularly passes our way is a holy man of God. Let us make a small roof chamber with walls, and put there for him a bed, a table, a chair, and a lamp, so that he can stay there whenever he comes to us.'" (2 Kgs 4:8–10)

**Reflection**: Many homes have an extra room which might be used as a part-time sewing room, play room, arts and crafts room, storage room, etc. It is often called the guest room. It is the room offered to relatives and friends who come to visit when that visit involves at least one night. Unlike the other more-furnished rooms of the home, the guest room sports the basic essentials, like a bed, a chair, and a lamp. In some homes, it may be accompanied by a private bathroom, but most likely whoever sleeps in it will have to share a bathroom with someone else.

In the guest room visitors are made to feel like they are in their own home. In the ancient world, that feeling was referred to as hospitality. The virtue of hospitality meant that one welcomed the visitor, the stranger, the pilgrim because such a person may be a messenger from God. Abraham learned that when he welcomed three strangers in the heat of the day and discovered that they were God bringing him the good news that he and Sarah would have a son.

Like we take leave of the other rooms of a house, it is good to take leave of the guest room. The unnamed woman of Shunem, a non-Israelite, recognized that Elisha, an Israelite, was a man of God. She not only welcomed him to her home, but she built a special guest room solely for his use. Later, on a return visit, Elisha offers the woman a precious gift: the awakening of her dead son.

**Activity**: Gather the members of the family in the guest room and ask each member to speak about a guest who has stayed there. Ask each family member to identify what gift the guest left for the family. Then, say the following prayer.

**Prayer**: Eternal God, you come to visit us in many ways. Do not let us fail to offer you hospitality. Help us to imitate the woman of Shunem and the hospitality of your servants Abraham and Sarah and welcome all who come our way. May the guest room in our new home be filled with guests even as this one has brought us many pilgrims through Jesus Christ our Lord. Amen.

**Leader**: Let us take leave of this guest bedroom in the peace of Christ.

**All**: Thanks be to God.

# The Den

**Scripture**: "[Jesus and his disciples] came to Jerusalem. And he entered the temple and began to drive out those who were selling and those who were buying in the temple, and he overturned the tables of the money changers and the seats of those who sold doves; and he would not allow anyone to carry anything through the temple. He was teaching and saying, 'Is it not written, "My house shall be called a house of prayer for all the nations"? But you have made it a den of robbers.'" (Mark 11:15–17)

**Reflection**: In the Bible, the word "den" seems to always carry a negative connotation, such as the lion's den, adder's den, den of jackals, or den of robbers. It indicates the lair of a predatory animal or a cave used as a hideout for secret activity. In the Bible a den does not connote the comfortable secluded room that we associate with it today.

For some people, the den in their home may be synonymous with the family room, but for others the den may be a place to relax and read or to listen to music, especially when the family room contains the TV. If there is a separate room referred to as the den, it is important for family members to take leave of it.

Jesus cleaned out the den of the temple. What the temple should have been—a den of prayer—had in effect become a marketplace, a den of commerce. In other words, the wrong activity was taking place in the temple. As the family members take leave of the den, they remember all the good things that took place there, depending on how the den was used. It may have been the place where books were read, where the paper was paged through, where family members gathered to speak about the things that really mattered to them in a comfortable and secluded atmosphere.

**Activity**: Gather the members of the family in the den and ask each member to remember and share an event, a conversation, a book, or something else that took place there. Then, say the following prayer.

**Prayer**: God of all life, you invite us into the den of your love and life. As we remember all that occurred in this den, help us to carry that spirit to the den of our new home. May every word spoken in confidence here be treasured by those who live in this house in the future. All praise be to you, our God, and your life-giving Spirit through your Son, our Lord Jesus Christ, now and for ever. Amen.

**Leader**: Let us take leave of this den in the peace of Christ.

**All**: Thanks be to God.

# The Bathroom

**Scripture**: "[Jesus said:] 'Do you not see that whatever goes into the mouth enters the stomach, and goes out into the sewer? But what comes out of the mouth proceeds from the heart, and this is what defiles. For out of the heart come evil intentions, murder, adultery, fornication, theft, false witness, slander. These are what defile a person . . . .'" (Matt 15:17–20)

**Reflection**: Some people think that the bathroom is the most important room in a house. In fact, its importance has grown from one in many older homes to one per bedroom in most new houses. The bathroom may be one of the few places that one can pray in private!

In the bathroom we eliminate both solid and liquid waste in the toilet. In the bathroom we shower or soak away dirt, grime, and oil in the tub. In the bathroom we shave or put on makeup. In the bathroom we prepare ourselves for the world.

So, it is wise to take leave of the bathroom, where children may have been potty trained, where women may have discovered a pregnancy, where men may have found a quiet moment to read the sport's page of the newspaper, where young adults may have taken the phone to speak privately to their first date. After all, it is a room that everyone uses several times a day for all kinds of activities.

**Activity**: Either gather the members of the family inside the bathroom, if it is large enough, or outside it, if it is too small. Place a small bowl of water in the center of your gathering place. Ask each member to share an important event he or she associates with the bathroom. After all have shared, pass around the bowl of water and invite each family member to remember his or her baptism by dipping his or her hand into the water and tracing the sign of the cross on his or her forehead. Then, say the following prayer.

**Prayer**: Caring God, you cleanse us in the waters of baptism and you remove from our hearts anything that can defile us. In this room we have been renewed and experienced your love. Help us to keep in memory all that has taken place here in the bathroom. In our new home make the bathroom a sacred place where we are renewed daily through Jesus Christ our Lord. Amen.

**Leader**: Let us take leave of this bathroom in the peace of Christ.

**All**: Thanks be to God.

# The Garage

**Scripture**: "When they had crossed [the Jordan River], Elijah said to Elisha, 'Tell me what I may do for you, before I am taken from you.' Elisha said, 'Please let me inherit a double share of your spirit.' He responded, 'You have asked a hard thing; yet, if you see me as I am being taken from you, it will be granted you; if not, it will not.' As they continued walking and talking, a chariot of fire and horses of fire separated the two of them, and Elijah ascended into a whirlwind into heaven." (2 Kgs 2:9–11)

**Reflection**: If the story of Elijah's ascent into heaven were being told today, he would get there in a Mercedes Benz, which would be backed out of a garage and into which he would seat himself and fasten his seat belt for the ride of his life! Or he would strap himself into a helicopter and whirl away toward the sun.

While many people use their garage for everything from a workshop to a storage room to a play room, it is designed to house the family chariot or car or SUV. And because that is its primary purpose, we take leave of it. It has provided protection for our primary means of transportation which itself has taken us wherever we wanted or had to go.

Our last trip will be in a vehicle from a church or funeral home to a cemetery or other place of rest. Unlike Elijah's ascent to heaven in a fiery chariot with fiery horses, ours will probably be a little more subdued. But, nevertheless, we need to say goodbye to the room which served so many purposes, the most important of which was protection of the family vehicle.

**Activity**: Gather the members of the family in the garage and ask each member either to narrate a memory of an event that took place in the garage or a memory that took place in the current or a past family vehicle. Then, say the following prayer.

**Prayer**: God of the journey, you accompanied your people, Israel, when they sojourned in the desert. You accompanied your prophets as they spoke your word to your people. As we remember the many events that took place in this garage, help us also to be aware of how you were present with us, leading and guiding us on our pilgrimage of faith. May we carry this faith with us to our new home where it will continue to grow through Jesus Christ our Lord. Amen.

**Leader**: Let us take leave of this garage in the peace of Christ.

**All**: Thanks be to God.

# The Sunroom

**Scripture**: ". . . Putting away falsehood let all of us speak the truth to our neighbors, for we are members of one another. Be angry but do not sin; do not let the sun go down on your anger, and do not make room for the devil." (Eph 4:25–27)

**Reflection**: The room is often referred to as a sunroom or a sun porch or a sun parlor. It is a glass enclosed room or porch with a sunny exposure. That means that it is a room filled with light, especially when the day is cloudless. Many homes have such rooms where family members read or relax or play together. Besides allowing in a lot of sunlight, a sunroom often features lots of living plants and maybe even a small water fountain. A sunroom is like an indoor garden in many ways.

The sunroom is a good place to remember all the light, both physical and spiritual, that has come to the members of the family. Most people thrive on light; some can barely survive without physical sunlight. Every member of the family also gives off light. That's why the author of the letter to the Ephesians exhorts his readers to speak the truth. When they do so, they shed light on each other, since they are members of one another. The author tells them not to let the sun go down on their anger; they are to make peace with each other in the light.

Taking leave of the sunroom offers the opportunity for family members to share how they have been light for each other, how they have been honest and truthful with each other, how they have respected each other, how they have honored each other in the light.

**Activity**: Gather the members of the family together in the sunroom and ask each person to share how another member has been light for him or her. Then, say the following prayer.

**Prayer**: God of light, you created the sun to be our light during the day and the moon to be our light during the night. We thank you for every good deed of light that has been done in this room and for every beam of light that members of this family have shone on each other. May we bear your light to our new home and shine it there wherever we discover darkness. We ask this through Jesus Christ our Lord, who is for ever the light of the world. Amen.

**Leader**: Let us take leave of this sunroom in the peace of Christ.

**All**: Thanks be to God.

## Going Away to College

**Scripture**: "Do not refrain from speaking at the proper moment, and do not hide your wisdom. For wisdom becomes known through speech, and education through the words of the tongue. Never speak against the truth, but be ashamed of your ignorance." (Sir 4:23–25)

**Reflection**: The first time a son or daughter leaves home for college can be a traumatic moment for both the young adult and his or her parents, especially if this is the first child or the last child to strike out on his or her own. The first child represents the trial run. Parents often do not reflect on what the young adult going away to college will mean for the whole family, especially if the person leaving has been helpful in running errands and shuttling younger siblings to games, appointments, and practices. If it is the last child to leave, parents are often not prepared for the resulting empty nest.

Watching a child pack clothes, an entertainment center, office supplies, and a day pack can make parents realize that a person they love will not reside permanently in the room he or she has occupied for eighteen years. The young adult becomes aware that he or she is leaving the security of the nest and must learn to fly on his or her own wings. A simple leave-taking ceremony on the day the young adult takes off for college can help all parties involved make a smooth transition to the weeks ahead.

The wisdom of Sirach urges us to speak about these things. A young adult listens to his or her parents and gains wisdom. Parents listen to the words of their young adult and get an education in return. What emerges from the dialogue is truth, especially when it comes to the fact that a person, who has been a part of a household, is leaving.

**Activity**: Parents and the young adult who is leaving gather in the child's room. Both parents share with the young man or woman several memories that they treasure of him or her growing up in the room. The young person shares several memories that he or she treasurers with his or her parents of growing up in the room. When all are finished, each person shares one thought about what this leaving for college means for him or her. Then, the following prayer is said.

**Prayer**: God of infinite knowledge, thank you for the words of instruction that you give us through the Bible and through each other. Help us to grow in your wisdom by listening attentively to all who teach us. Be with and guide N. as he/she leaves this room today. May he/she treasure the education he/she will receive and always speak the truth through Jesus Christ our Lord. Amen.

**Leader**: Let us take leave of this room in the peace of Christ.

**All**: Thanks be to God.

*chapter two*

## Quickly Taking Leave of One's Home

There are occasions when one must leave his or her home quickly, and there is no time to take leave over several weeks or even several days. If such is your case, choose one of the following leave-taking rituals and celebrate it with as many members of your family as possible. Even if you have to mark the taking leave of your home alone, it is important for you to acknowledge that you are moving. After a few moments of prayer, take leave of your home.

# Poor Health

**Scripture**: "Better off poor, healthy, and fit than rich and afflicted in body. Health and fitness are better than any gold and a robust body than countless riches. There is no wealth better than health of body, and no gladness above joy of heart." (Sir 30:14–16)

**Reflection**: The wisdom of Sirach, sometimes referred to as Ecclesiasticus, makes us realize how important good health is. The sad part is that we don't often recognize Sirach's wisdom concerning well-being until we find ourselves in poor health, gradually deteriorating because of one or any number of diseases.

Poor health often forces people to leave their homes quickly and move to a retirement center, a child's home, an assisted living center, or a skilled nursing center. Such a move may be voluntary or involuntary, depending on the person and the situation. But a transition from one place of residence to another is required, and taking leave of one's home and possessions can make the move a little easier.

In times of poor health, periods of insecurity, we tend to cling to what is ours because it gives us a sense of security and stability. The prospect of moving places us in a deeper state of chaos, especially if we are not able to control the process of moving. Taking leave of our home and possessions can help to restore a little order in the chaos.

**Activity**: Before leaving your home (for the last time) either speak to other family members or, if you are able, make a list of your fondest memories of living in your house and share those with family members and friends in your new place of residence. In either case, record these memories in a journal and designate that journal as a gift to a family member at the time of your death. Then, say the following prayer.

**Prayer**: God of the poor and the rich, I give you thanks for the joy of heart that I have enjoyed living in my home. Thank you for all the good health that I have enjoyed over the years. If it is your will, gracious God, restore me to health. If not, give me the peace of your Holy Spirit through Jesus Christ my Lord. Amen.

**Leader:** Let us (me) take leave of this home in the peace of Christ.

**All:** Thanks be to God.

# Health Emergency

**Scripture:** "Pleasant words are like a honeycomb, sweetness to the soul and health to the body. Sometimes there is a way that seems to be right, but in the end it is the way to death." (Prov 16:24–25)

**Reflection:** One minute we are doing fine, and the next minute we find ourselves in the emergency room after having a heart attack, a stroke, or taking a fall. Because of some other serious condition, we might also find ourselves in the recovery room after having had emergency surgery. Because of our health emergency, we cannot go home again right now, and other living arrangements need to be made.

The wise words of Proverbs can be a help in making a transition from our home to another place to live. Pleasant words can sweeten the experience, especially if those pleasant words center on the memories we carry with us from our home. While we can move ourselves out of our home, we cannot move our memories out of ourselves; thoughts are ours for ever.

While we might at first refuse to leave our home—the only course of action that seems to be right—Proverbs warns us that stance may end in our death. After a health emergency, when we can no longer go home and take care of ourselves and must move to a new permanent place where we can get the care we need, we also must take leave of our home, remembering the pleasant words spoken there.

**Activity:** Before permanently leaving your home either speak to other family members or, if you are able, make a list of the most pleasant words ever spoken in your home and share those with family members and friends in your new place of residence. In either case, record these memories in a journal and designate that journal as a gift to a family member at the time of your death. Then, say the following prayer.

**Prayer**: Mighty God, ever-present physician of body and soul, with pleasant words you offer comfort to your people when they face medical emergencies. As I take leave of my home, remind me of all the pleasant words spoken within its walls. Help me to take the sweetness of those words with me to my new home through Jesus Christ my Lord. Amen.

**Leader**: Let us (me) take leave of this home in the peace of Christ.

**All**: Thanks be to God.

# Age

**Scripture**: "When Israel [Jacob] saw Joseph's sons, he said, 'Who are these?' Joseph said to his father, 'They are my sons, whom God has given me here' [in Egypt]. And he said, 'Bring them to me, please, that I may bless them.' Now the eyes of Israel were dim with age, and he could not see well. So Joseph brought them near him; and he kissed them and embraced them." (Gen 48:8–10)

**Reflection**: When we are young children, we count days and weeks and months instead of years. Later in our childhood, we cannot wait to grow up; reaching twenty-one seems to be a goal that takes for ever. In our early adulthood years, we look at those who are thirty or forty years of age and think about how old they are! Then, when we hit forty, we realize how old forty is not! Gradually, we make our transition to fifty, a crisis point in life for many who wait to come to terms with their mortality. Then come retirement and, finally, our post-retirement years.

We cannot stop getting older. Ageing is a fact of life. We keep count of how many times we have been around the sun while keeping our feet planted somewhere on planet Earth. Ageing, no matter if we live to seventy, eighty, ninety, or even one hundred years, inevitably brings us to our death. When we cannot take care of ourselves or our home in our older years, we have to leave our house behind and move to new place for assisted living or skilled nursing care.

With age comes wisdom, not necessarily knowledge, but a wealth of experiences to be shared with others. That's what Jacob (Israel) recognized in his grandsons, Joseph's children. Jacob wanted to bless them with the wisdom of his years. Even though he could no longer see well, Jacob wanted to share all that God had done in his life with his grandsons. Before we take leave of our home in our older years, it is a wise endeavor to share our wisdom with our children, our grandchildren, and friends.

**Activity**: Before taking leaving your home with the help of a trusted family member or friend, make a list of the members of your family and your special friends. After the name of each write what words of wisdom you want to share with each person. Then, after the move, find a way to share that wisdom with each individual through a letter, a postcard, e-mail, or conversation. If you are not able to write, make it a point, nevertheless, to give a few words of wisdom to each family member and friend as part of taking leave of your home. Say the following prayer.

**Prayer**: God of all ages, you brought me to birth through my parents and nourished me with your grace as I grew in your presence. Throughout my life, you have sustained me as I have continued my pilgrimage to you. Be with me now as I take leave of my home. Help me to share the wisdom that you have taught me with the members of my family and my friends. Then, at the end of my years grant that I may share life with you for ever through Jesus Christ my Lord. Amen.

**Leader**: Let us (me) take leave of this home in the peace of Christ.

**All**: Thanks be to God.

## Sudden Death of a Spouse

**Scripture**: "Sarah lived one hundred twenty-seven years; this was the length of Sarah's life. . . . And Abraham went in to mourn for Sarah and to weep for her. After this, Abraham buried Sarah his wife in the cave of the field of Machpelah facing Mamre (that is, Hebron) in the land of Canaan." (Gen 23:1–2, 19)

**Reflection**: Either after raising children, watching them leave home and carve out lives for themselves, and living alone for several years, or after having no children, a spouse dies and the living spouse discovers that he or she must leave the home because of age, finances, loneliness, etc. Abraham faced this challenge after the death of his wife, Sarah. He purchased a field with a cave in it and buried his beloved spouse there. Then, he had to move on. Of course, since Abraham lived in a tent, taking down the tent was a little easier than preparing to move a lifetime of possessions.

The sudden death of a spouse spins the living into a whirl of chaos. Taking care of the funeral arrangements is chaos enough, let alone trying to decide what to do next. Many survivors take a few months to mourn their loss and to be sure that they are thinking clearly before they decide to move. Others, because they cannot take care of themselves, because they cannot afford to do so, because of the fear of living alone, etc. decide to move immediately. After making such a decision, one needs to take leave of his or her home.

Taking leave of a home alone after the death of a spouse means that the survivor must sort through not only his or her possessions, but the dead partner's things and the items both owned together. Not only can this assist in the grieving process, but it can enable a peaceful leave-taking. Sometimes the survivor may want to do this alone, and other times he or she may seek the assistance of a family member or close friend. Whatever the case, leaving one's home after the death of a spouse can be done with grace as the survivor reverently sorts through a lifetime of possessions.

**Activity**: While sorting through your possessions, your deceased spouse's possessions, and the things you owned together, pick three items that hold special memories. Either share those memories with the person assisting you or record those memories in a journal. You might want to give specific items to members of your family and to share the memory you attach to the item with the family member. That way you entrust not only items but memories to others. After sharing, say the following prayer.

**Prayer**: God of all memory, you never forget any of your children, especially those who have left this world. Remember my deceased spouse, N., and grant him/her the joy of your presence. As I take leave of this house and distribute my memories to my family members and friends, help me to keep the memory of my spouse alive in my heart until I come to share in your eternal life through Jesus Christ my Lord. Amen.

**Leader**: Let us (me) take leave of this home in the peace of Christ.

**All**: Thanks be to God.

# Financial Reasons

**Scripture**: "Keep your lives free from the love of money, and be content with what you have; for [God] has said, 'I will never leave you or forsake you.' So we can say with confidence, 'The Lord is my helper; I will not be afraid. What can anyone do to me?'" (Heb 13:5–6)

**Reflection**: There comes a point where we have to say to ourselves that we can no longer financially afford something. It might be the cost of cable TV, the cost of medical care, the cost of keeping a car running, etc. While the Bible frequently exhorts us to be aware of the love of money, the fact is that we need money to survive. And often for financial reasons we cannot continue to live in our home and must move to less-expensive place to live, such as with an adult child or friend, an apartment, assisted living, retirement center, or other type of home. Being forced to move because of personal finances is a traumatic realization and experience, especially if we have been financially secure for most of our lives.

While we leave a home, the author of Hebrews reminds us that we do not leave God. God promises never to leave or forsake us. God promises to help us. So, we do not have to fear while we take leave of our home. Especially if we understand that this is the next step of our lifetime journey, we can find comfort in God being with us as we travel to a new home.

In the midst of moving, we can focus on the contentment we have experienced in our home. When we begin to think about it, there have been many moments of contentment, feelings of satisfaction with our possessions, our status, and our situation. Those moments of contentment have kept us free from the love of money. Furthermore, those moments of contentment can reveal to us how God was quietly working in our lives.

**Activity**: Recall some of the moments of contentment you have experienced in your home. If that seems too general, think of a moment of contentment in each room of your house. What was God revealing to you in that moment? Either share your moments of contentment with the other members of your family or record them in a journal and designate its owner at the time of your death. Say the following prayer.

**Prayer**: Eternal God, you give us days and months and years to serve you. As I remember all the moments of contentment and reflect upon all you have done in my life in this house, make be grateful for all your acts through me and my life. As I move from here, give me the grace to trust you more deeply and to follow you more faithfully through Jesus Christ my Lord. Amen.

**Leader**: Let us (me) take leave of this home in the peace of Christ.

**All**: Thanks be to God.

# Job Transfer

**Scripture:** "Ruth said, 'Do not press me to leave you or to turn back from following you! Where you go, I will go; where you lodge, I will lodge; your people shall be my people and your God my God. Where you die, I will die—there will I be buried . . . .' When Naomi saw that [Ruth] was determined to go with her, she said no more to her. . . . [T]he two of them went on until they came to Bethlehem." (Ruth 1:16–19)

**Reflection:** Sometimes we have to leave a home because of a job transfer. For a single person, this is difficult; for a married couple with children and so many people to accommodate this can look like impossibility. One member of the family often moves and searches for a new home while the other members stay behind to finish a school year or a semester, to tie up loose ends, and to pack in preparation for the move. With one family member already moved out because of a job transfer this can be a very stressful time for all.

Ruth refused to leave Naomi, so the two women moved on together. Likewise, when a job is at stake, one or several members of a family often refuse to leave the other members. It is very difficult for children to say good-bye to their friends and classmates, especially if they have attended a school for a long time. It is painful for couples to leave behind their circle of friends and support communities which have nourished them through the years. But such taking leave has to be done. Without saying good-bye to some people we cannot say hello to other persons.

When a move is sparked by a job transfer, if the whole family can't move at once, it is important that the transferee participate in the family leave-taking of the home by being present for some of the process, such as using some of the reflections in chapter 1. At minimum, the person moving ahead of the others should be sent on his or her way using the following activity.

**Activity:** Either a few days before, the day before, or a few hours before the person with the new job leaves, the family members gather together. Each shares a memory that is important to him or her about living in the home with the member leaving. After the sharing, all gather around the member leaving and pray.

**Prayer:** God of our journeys, we give you thanks for all the memories we have shared in this home and for the life you have given us here. Bless N. as he/she goes ahead of us to work and to find a new home in which we will live. Guide his/her trip and search. Reunite us as a family soon and give us the grace to continue our pilgrimage to you through Jesus Christ our Lord. Amen.

**Leader:** Let N. take leave of this home in the peace of Christ.

**All:** Thanks be to God.

# Alone and Can't Care for Self

**Scripture:** "Jesus said, 'The hour is coming, indeed it has come, when you will be scattered, each one to his home, and you will leave me alone. Yet I am not alone because the Father is with me. I have said this to you, so that in me you may have peace . . . .'" (John 16:31–33)

**Reflection:** For whatever the reason—health, disease, trauma, age, finances, etc.—people find themselves alone and unable to take care of themselves adequately and they must move to where there are others who can care for them, such as the home of a family member, an assisted living center, or a skilled nursing center. For some people this seems to occur over night. In other words, it creeps up on them.

When such a scenario presents itself and before a move occurs, a simple leave-taking ceremony should be held. At this point in most people's lives, they have no control over what is happening to them. Leave-taking can assist them in having some control over the move and enable them to do it with grace. Even Jesus knew that he would one day be left alone except for God. By telling his disciples that he would be left alone, Jesus empowered them with peace.

Someone who is unable to care for himself or herself needs to be empowered with the peace that he or she still has some input concerning the move. This can be accomplished by seeking the person's assistance in determining what to take to the new home, what to give to whom, and what to sell in a garage sale. The best course of action is not to assume that one knows another's wishes, but to ask him or her about what plans he or she has for the major items in the home.

**Activity**: Gather together the members of the family along with the person who can no longer care for himself or herself either in the home from which one is moving or in another place. Ask the person what his or her plans are for the major items in the home. Family members listen and record what the person says. They ask about any major things not mentioned, and they assure the person moving that his or her wishes will be acted upon. When finished, they say the following prayer.

**Prayer**: Mighty God, you are always present with us, and you never leave us unattended. Even when Jesus, your Son, felt alone, you did not abandon him but strengthened him for his mission of spreading your good news throughout the world. Be with us here as we help N. take leave of his/her home. Be with him/her in the move and strengthen all of us in our journey to you through Jesus Christ our Lord. Amen.

**Leader**: Let us take leave of this home in the peace of Christ.

**All**: Thanks be to God.

# When One Can't Go Back Home

**Scripture**: "In the time of plenty think of the time of hunger; in days of wealth think of poverty and need. From morning to evening conditions change; all things move swiftly before the Lord. One who is wise is cautious in everything . . . ." (Sir 18:25–27)

**Reflection**: Change is inevitable, yet people fight it and hold on to the past. As the wisdom of Sirach states, just from the morning to the evening things change. But note that Sirach says that they change before God, who is watching over and guiding this always-in-flux world which the Holy One created. We should not fear change, but should embrace it since we are a part of creation.

There are times when a person must move because he or she cannot go back home again. This may be occasioned by a medical condition, an accident, some incapacity, etc. Something keeps a person from going home and preparing to move. When such an occasion presents itself, it is important for some type of leave-taking to occur to ensure that a smooth transition from one home to another is brought about. As Sirach states, the wise person is cautious in everything. The wise person will be sure that the person who can't go home again is given the opportunity to take leave of his or her home.

**Activity**: Gather the members of the family in the new home of the person who can't go home again. With the person each family member shares a memory that he or she has of the home. The person who can't go home again should be given the opportunity to request that several items that are the dearest to him or her be brought to him or her, and he or she shares a memory triggered by each item that has been a part of his or her home. Those items should be given a special place in the new home. Then, the following prayer is said.

**Prayer**: Lord God, you are eternal, a never-changing spirit who unfolds your plan in human time. Through our sharing of these memories, strengthen us in your service and guide us in our pilgrimage to you. Make us grateful for your many gifts and make us wise enough to know the ways of your Son, Jesus, and follow him faithfully for ever and ever. Amen.

**Leader:** Let us take leave of N's. home in the peace of Christ.

**All:** Thanks be to God.

## Armed Forces Call or Enlistment

**Scripture:** "For everything there is a season, and a time for every matter under heaven: a time to be born, and a time to die; . . . a time to kill, and a time to heal; . . . a time to love, and a time to hate; a time for war, and a time for peace." (Eccl 3:1–3, 8)

**Reflection:** When a person enlists or already belongs to a branch of the armed forces of a country or the reserves, he or she may be called to service suddenly, especially at the time of the threat of war or during war. That may mean that other members of the family have to move for financial, social, or security reasons. A spouse left behind may feel more secure moving back home to his or her parents' house. A spouse with children may need the help of the members of his or her extended family and move to be closer to them. When a move is occasioned by a call to duty in the armed services, there is little time to take leave of the home.

The author of Ecclesiastes reminds us that there is a season and a time for everything. Just because we don't realize what is taking place, or because our field of vision is too narrow, Ecclesiastes reminds us that the picture is always bigger than we think. There is no time for God; all is part of the Holy One's eternal plan and our small part in it. As a popular cliché puts it, we should just go with the flow.

In the midst of the chaos of moving and seeing a loved one off to serve his or her country, we need to take leave of our home, no matter if we have lived there for a few years or several months. Paraphrasing Ecclesiastes, there is a time to move, and a time to stay. During the time of preparing to move, reminding ourselves that this move is one more revelation of God's plan for us may give us some comfort.

**Activity**: After gathering the members of the family together, ask each one to share one memory that each treasures about living in the home. After all have shared, ask each to write that memory on a single sheet of paper. Gather the pages and give them to the person who is going to serve his or her country. That will enable him or her to remember living in this home. Then, say the following prayer.

**Prayer**: God of all time, you reveal your will for us throughout the ages. You bring us to birth, and you comfort us through death. You guide our steps to where you want us to be in each stage of our lives. Be with N., who goes to serve his/her country. May the memories of this home remain with him/her and with all of us who prepare to move. Bring us together again in a time of peace through Jesus Christ our Lord. Amen.

**Leader**: Let us take leave of this home in the peace of Christ.

**All**: Thanks be to God.

# chapter three

## Taking Leave of One's Home
## after a Disaster

There are occasions when one must leave his or her home because it has been destroyed in a disaster, such as a tornado, earthquake, or fire. If such is your case, choose one of the following leave-taking rituals and celebrate it with as many members of your family as possible near the place where your home stood or on the site where it was built. Even if you have to mark the taking leave of your home alone, it is important for you to acknowledge that you are moving. After a few moments of prayer, take leave of your home.

# Tornado/Wind

**Scripture**: "A great windstorm arose, and the waves beat into the boat, so that the boat was already being swamped. But [Jesus] was in the stern, asleep on the cushion; and [the disciples] woke him up and said to him, 'Teacher, do you not care that we are perishing?' He woke up and rebuked the wind, and said to the sea, 'Peace! Be Still!' Then the wind ceased, and there was a dead calm." (Mark 4:37–39)

**Reflection**: If one lives in the heartland of the United States, tornado warnings are a part of daily life from early spring through late fall. Hundreds occur every year, yet few do damage because they touch down in the middle of a field on the plains of Texas, Oklahoma, Kansas, Nebraska, Arkansas, Missouri, or other states forming the mid-section of the country. The black funnel cloud twists its way across the land and disappears as mysteriously as it appeared.

Sometimes homes are partially or totally destroyed by tornadoes or strong winds. However, not only is the home in chaos, but the members of the family who lived in it are also deeply disturbed about the loss of their home. The words of Jesus calming the wind and the sea might offer some comfort and stillness in the midst of the feelings of being swamped and not being able to see the next step that needs to be taken.

A natural disaster, such as a tornado, reminds us that we are not always in control of our lives or our property. Nature has her own way, and we try to live with her. The bottom line is that the Creator never leaves us alone. In the midst of every storm, no matter how strong, God is with us stilling the wind and offering us some peace. The dead calm that can ensue after taking leave of our home can serve as assurance of God's presence with us even through disaster.

**Activity**: After gathering the members of the family near the home, if there is some remaining, or on the site of the home, if it has been destroyed—or, if neither of those is possible, in another place—ask each family member to share several memories of events marked in the home. After all have shared, ask each member to share how this has helped him or her reach a moment of peace. Ask someone either to write or to record these memories. Take the written or recorded memories with you to your new home. Say the following prayer.

**Prayer**: Lord God, from the east and the west, from the north and the south, you make your presence felt with the wind. At this time of disaster, strengthen our resolve as we take leave of this home. Bless all who have lived here. Bless the memories we take from here. With your Spirit guide us to a new home where we can find calm and peace through Jesus Christ our Lord. Amen.

**Leader**: Let us take leave of this home in the peace of Christ.

**All**: Thanks be to God.

# Flood

**Scripture**: "Jesus said: '. . . Everyone who hears these words of mine and does not act on them will be like a foolish man who built his house on sand. The rain fell, and the floods came, and the winds blew and beat against that house, and it fell—and great was its fall!'" (Matt 7:26–27)

**Reflection**: Those who build or move into homes already built near rivers, dams, and levees can enjoy the beauty of those bodies of water until the rivers crest their banks, the dams spill over, and the levees break. Add the threat of the ocean to those who build on its shore and we know how powerful a flood can be. Every year many homes are destroyed by floods all over the world.

In Matthew's Gospel, Jesus uses the metaphor of a house built on rock to communicate to his hearers the importance of building themselves on solid teaching. Those who ignore his teaching are like fools who build houses on sand. When the flood comes, the sand gives way, and the house is destroyed. But the physical destruction of a home does not imply the destruction of a family. After a flood the family members must take leave of their home and move to another home.

Keep in mind that family is built on rock. It can withstand the flood of change and turn this experience of disaster into one of growth. Only the physical house has been destroyed by the flood; the ties that bind together the members of the family cannot be washed away easily.

**Activity**: After gathering the members of the family near the home, if there is some remaining, or on the site of the home, if it has been destroyed—or, if neither of those is possible, in another place—ask each family member to share several memories of events marked in the home. Ask someone either to write or to record these memories. Then, ask each member to share how he or she has been strengthened through the sharing. Take the written or recorded memories with you to your new home. Say the following prayer.

**Prayer**: God of power and might, you never abandon your people in their time of need. Be with us now as we take leave of our home. May we always know your presence in our lives when the rivers of life's problems threaten to overflow their banks. Grant that the memories we carry with us from this home to our new home will further strengthen our love for each other through Jesus Christ our Lord. Amen.

**Leader**: Let us take leave of this home in the peace of Christ.

**All**: Thanks be to God.

# Earthquake

**Scripture**: ". . . Jesus cried . . . with a loud voice and breathed his last. . . . The earth shook, and the rocks were split. Now when the centurion and those with him, who were keeping watch over Jesus, saw the earthquake and what took place, they were terrified . . ." (Matt 27:50–51, 54)

**Reflection:** In the ancient world, an earthquake was considered to be the occasion for divine revelation. So, the author of Matthew's Gospel uniquely uses the earthquake in his story of Jesus' death and again in his story of the empty tomb. While others are afraid, those who believe that God often speaks through earthquakes, like the author of Matthew's Gospel, know that God is revealing the Holy One's power.

Today, we know that earthquakes are caused by the shifting and bumping or rubbing together of tectonic plates, huge geological structures that form the crust of the third planet from the sun. Those places where plates shift or bump or rub together are called faults. Homes built near or on faults often are destroyed when high-powered earthquakes occur.

When a home is destroyed by an earthquake, the family needs to take leave of it. But the members of the family can also come to realize that the God who was with them in their home before the earthquake will be with them in their new home after the earthquake. That's essentially the message of Matthew's Gospel: God does not abandon people in need. God walks with them through the shaking to the quiet and new life on the other side.

**Activity:** After gathering the members of the family near the home, if there is some remaining, or on the site of the home, if it has been destroyed—or, if neither of those is possible, in another place—ask each family member to share several memories of events marked in the home. After all have shared several memories, ask each to share how he or she recognized God's presence in the old home. Ask someone either to write or to record these memories. Take the written or recorded memories with you to your new home. Say the following prayer.

**Prayer:** Father of Jesus, you announced the good news of the resurrection of your Son, Jesus, with an earthquake. As we take leave of this home destroyed by an earthquake, make us aware of the new life that you are awakening in each of us. May our memories strengthen us in our move and help us to recognize even deeper your presence in our lives. Hear our prayer through Jesus Christ our Lord. Amen.

**Leader**: Let us take leave of this home in the peace of Christ.

**All**: Thanks be to God.

# Fire

**Scripture**: "The LORD went in front of [the Hebrews] in a pillar of cloud by day, to lead them along the way, and in a pillar of fire by night, to give them light, so that they might travel by day and by night. Neither the pillar of cloud by day nor the pillar of fire by night left its place in front of the people." (Exod 13:21–22)

**Reflection**: While there is no doubt that fire is destructive, in the Hebrew Bible's Book of Exodus fire is a sign of God's guiding presence. The Mighty One is the leader of the Hebrew people's escape from Egyptian slavery. In order to keep them on the move to get as far away from their taskmasters as possible, God shows the way with fire by night and cloud by day. And the people follow.

When a home is destroyed by fire, those who have lived in it need to take leave of it. While there may be little or nothing left, the leave-taking can enable the family members who lived there to identify God leading them to a new home. Awakening all to the presence of God can help to bring some solace in the midst of such disaster.

Moses encounters God's presence in the form of a flame of fire out of a bush which commissions Moses to take a leadership role in getting the Hebrews ready to leave Egypt. At first Moses is reluctant, but God's flame warms his heart and sets him on fire with his mission. The flame that destroyed a home can serve as the spark that sets in motion a family's move to a new home. In other words, it seems that in the Bible God always guides people to new and more abundant life.

**Activity**: After gathering the members of the family near the home, if there is some remaining, or on the site of the home, if it has been destroyed—or, if neither of those is possible, in another place—ask each family member to share several memories of events marked in the home. After all have shared several memories, ask each to share what he or she needs now from other members to make the move to a new home. Ask someone either to write or to record these memories. Take the written or recorded memories with you to your new home. Say the following prayer.

**Prayer**: God of day and night, you watch over us constantly and guide us in your ways. As we take leave of this home destroyed by fire, lead us to a new home. Put into the heart of each member of our family the flame of your Holy Spirit. Lead us in our mission to find a new home and strengthen us in your service through Jesus Christ our Lord. Amen.

**Leader**: Let us take leave of this home in the peace of Christ.

**All**: Thanks be to God.

# Snow/Ice/Hail/Avalanche

**Scripture**: "In [the Lord's] majesty he gives the clouds their strength, and the hailstones are broken in pieces. The voice of his thunder rebukes the earth; when he appears, the mountains shake. At his will the south wind blows; so the storm from the north and the whirlwind. He scatters the snow like birds flying down, and its descent is like locusts alighting. The eye is dazzled by the beauty of its whiteness, and the mind is amazed as it falls." (Sir 43:15–18)

**Reflection**: In the wise reflections of Sirach, we find a tone of wonder at the elements of a snowstorm: clouds, sleet, snowflakes, and the brightness of the sun reflected off of the newly fallen snow. But such is not what we see when a home has been destroyed by snow, ice, hail, or avalanche. The dazzling ways of nature become heartbreak for members of a family.

Taking leave of a home destroyed by nature is not easy. The question Why? lingers on the edge of every family member. While no definitive answer can ever be given, participating in a leave-taking ceremony can put the disaster into perspective and help all cope with it. The awful tragedy can be seen within the perspective of the awful beauty of nature.

It is difficult to look at any aspect of nature and not simultaneously see its beauty and tragedy. A river is a sight to behold, but when it breaks its banks, it destroys. Fire gathers us together, but when it escapes its ring or place, it consumes everything it touches. Likewise, snow, ice, hail, or avalanche manifests the elegance of nature, but they can also gracefully destroy whatever gets in their path. That's the paradoxical character of snow; it manifests the paradoxical character of the God who created it.

**Activity**: After gathering the members of the family near the home, if there is some remaining, or on the site of the home, if it has been destroyed—or, if neither of those is possible, in another place—ask each family member to share several memories of events marked in the home. After all have shared several memories, ask each to share how the paradoxical character of snow manifests the paradoxical character of God. Ask someone either to write or to record these memories. Take the written or recorded memories with you to your new home. Say the following prayer.

**Prayer**: God of heaven and earth, winter is one of your gifts to your people. As we take leave of this home destroyed by winter's fury, scatter your grace upon us. Strengthen us through our sharing and guide us to the security of our new home. May we come to appreciate more deeply the awful beauty of all that you have created through Jesus Christ our Lord. Amen.

**Leader**: Let us take leave of this home in the peace of Christ.

**All**: Thanks be to God.

# *chapter four*

## Taking Leave of the Home
## on Moving Day

This is the final prayer that should be conducted in the home on moving day. Gather the family and any who are assisting in the move into one of the empty rooms of the home.

**Leader**: Let us begin in the name of the Father, and of the Son, and of the Holy Spirit. (All make the sign of the cross with the leader.)

**All**: Amen.

**Leader**: Peace to this house and all who have lived here.

**All**: And with your spirit.

# Introduction

**Leader**: John's Gospel tells us that God the Word, Christ, became flesh and lived among us. While he made the earth his home, the Word was known as Jesus of Nazareth, born of Mary. Those who have lived in this home have experienced the blessings and presence of God the Word within it. God has nurtured the members of this family's love for each other here, shared in their joys, and comforted them in their sorrows. From this home, the N. family has carried God's blessings to others. Now, as the family members take leave of this home, they ask for a peaceful leave-taking and a safe move to a new home.

# Reading

*One of the six following biblical texts is chosen and read by a member of the family.*

1

*Genesis 12:1–5, 7–8 (Abraham is called to leave his home.)*

A reading from the Book of Genesis:

Now the LORD said to Abram, "Go from your country and your kindred and your father's house to the land that I will show you. I will make of you a great nation, and I will bless you, and make your name great, so that you will be a blessing. I will bless those who bless you, and the one who curses you I will curse; and in you all the families of the earth shall be blessed."

# Taking Leave of Your Home

So Abram went, as the LORD had told him; and Lot went with him. Abram was seventy-five years old when he departed from Haran. Abram took his wife Sarai and his brother's son Lot, and all the possessions that they had gathered, and the persons whom they had acquired in Haran; and they set forth to go to the land of Canaan.

Then the LORD appeared to Abram, and said, "To your off-spring I will give this land." So he built there an altar to the LORD, who had appeared to him. From there he moved on to the hill country on the east of Bethel, and pitched his tent . . . ; and there he built an altar to the LORD and invoked the name of the LORD. The word of the Lord.

**All**: Thanks be to God.

2

*Exodus 33:1–3, 7–11a, 13–14, 17 (God promises Moses that the Lord will be with the people.)*

A reading from the Book of Exodus:

The LORD said to Moses, "Go, leave this place, you and the people whom you have brought up out of the land of Egypt, and go to the land of which I swore to Abraham, Isaac, and Jacob, say-ing, 'To your descendants I will give it.' I will send an angel before you. . . . Go up to a land flowing with milk and honey. . . ."

Now Moses used to take the tent and pitch it outside the camp, far off from the camp; he called it the tent of meeting. And everyone who sought the LORD would go out to the tent of meet-ing, which was outside the camp. Whenever Moses went out to the tent, all the people would rise and stand, each of them, at the entrance of their tents and watch Moses until he had gone into the tent. When Moses entered the tent, the pillar of cloud would descend and stand at the entrance of the tent, and the LORD would speak with Moses. When all the people saw the pillar of cloud standing at the entrance of the tent, all the people would rise and bow down, all of them, at the entrance of their tent. Thus the LORD used to speak to Moses face to face, as one speaks to a friend.

Moses said to the LORD, "Now if I have found favor in your sight, show me your ways, so that I may know you and find favor in your sight. Consider too that this nation is your people." He said, "My presence will go with you, and I will give you rest. . . . I will do the very thing that you have asked; for you have found favor in my sight, and I know you by name."
The word of the Lord.

**All**: Thanks be to God.


3

*Numbers 10:11–13, 33–34 (The Israelites leave the wilderness by stages.)*

A reading from the Book of Numbers:

In the second year, in the second month, on the twentieth day of the month, the cloud lifted from over the tabernacle of the covenant. Then the Israelites set out by stages from the wilderness of Sinai, and the cloud settled down in the wilderness of Paran. They set out for the first time at the command of the LORD by Moses.

So they set out from the mount of the LORD three days' journey with the ark of the covenant of the LORD going before them three days' journey, to seek out a resting place for them, the cloud of the LORD being over them by day when they set out from the camp.
The word of the Lord.

**All**: Thanks be to God.


4

*1 Kings 19:4–9 (Elijah is strengthened for his journey.)*

A reading from the First Book of Kings:

[Elijah] went a day's journey into the wilderness, and came and sat down under a solitary broom tree. He asked that he might die: "It is enough; now, O LORD, take away my life, for I am no better than my ancestors." Then he lay down under the broom tree and fell asleep. Suddenly an angel touched him and said to him, "Get up and eat." He looked, and there at his head was a cake baked on hot stones, and a jar of water. He ate and drank, and lay down again.

The angel of the LORD came a second time, touched him, and said, "Get up and eat, otherwise the journey will be too much for you." He got up, and ate and drank; then he went in the strength of that food forty days and forty nights to Horeb the mount of God. At that place he came to a cave, and spent the night there. The word of the Lord.

**All**: Thanks be to God.

5

*Tobit 5:16–18, 22–23 (Raphael agrees to accompany Tobias on his journey.)*

A reading from the Book of Tobit:

Tobit said to Raphael, ". . . Go with my son [Tobias], and I will add something to your wages." Raphael answered, "I will go with him; so do not fear. We shall leave in good health and return to you in good health, because the way is safe." So Tobit said to him, "Blessings be upon you, brother."

Then he called his son and said to him, "Son, prepare supplies for the journey and set out with your brother. May God in heaven bring you safely there and return you in good health to me; and may his angel, my son, accompany you both for your safety." Before he went out to start his journey, he kissed his father and mother. Tobit then said to him, "Have a safe journey."

But his mother began to weep, and said to Tobit, "Why is it that you have sent my child away? Is he not the staff of our hand as he goes in and out before us?" Tobit said to her, "Do not worry;

our child will leave in good health and return to us in good health. Your eyes will see him on the day when he returns to you in good health. Say no more! Do not fear for them, my sister. For a good angel will accompany him; his journey will be successful, and he will come back in good health."

The word of the Lord.

**All**: Thanks be to God.

## 6

*Wisdom 18:1–3 (God guides the Israelites.)*

A reading from the Book of Wisdom:

. . . For your holy ones, God, there was very great light. Their enemies heard their voices but did not see their forms, and counted them happy for not having suffered, and were thankful that your holy ones, though previously wronged, were doing them no injury; and they begged their pardon for having been at variance with them.

Therefore you provided a flaming pillar of fire as a guide for your people's unknown journey, and a harmless sun for their glorious wandering.

The word of the Lord.

**All**: Thanks be to God.

# Psalm Response
*One of the three following Psalms is recited by all.*

## 1

*Psalm 8*

O LORD, our Sovereign,
    how majestic is your name in all the earth!

# Taking Leave of Your Home

You have set your glory above the heavens.
    Out of the mouths of babes and infants
you have founded a bulwark because of your foes,
    to silence the enemy and the avenger.

When I look at your heavens, the work of your fingers,
    the moon and the stars that you have established;
what are human beings that you are mindful of them,
    mortals that you care for them?

Yet you have made them a little lower than God,
    and crowned them with glory and honor.
You have given them dominion over the works of your hands;
    you have put all things under their feet,
all sheep and oxen,
    and also the beasts of the field,
the birds of the air, and the fish of the sea,
    whatever passes along the paths of the seas.

O LORD, our Sovereign,
    how majestic is your name in all the earth!


2

*Psalm 54:1–4, 6–7*

Save me, O God, by your name, and vindicate me by your might.
Hear my prayer, O God; give ear to the words of my mouth.
For the insolent have risen against me, the ruthless seek my life;
    they do not set God before them.
But surely, God is my helper; the Lord is the upholder of my life.
With a freewill offering I will sacrifice to you;
    I will give thanks to your name, O LORD, for it is good.
For he has delivered me from every trouble,
    and my eye has looked in triumph on my enemies.

3

*Psalm 112*

Praise the LORD!
Happy are those who fear the LORD,
    who greatly delight in his commandments.
Their descendants will be mighty in the land;
    the generation of the upright will be blessed.
Wealth and riches are in their houses,
    and their righteousness endures forever.
They rise in the darkness as a light for the upright;
    they are gracious, merciful, and righteous.
It is well with those who deal generously and lend,
    who conduct their affairs with justice.
For the righteous will never be moved;
    they will be remembered forever.
They are not afraid of evil tidings;
    their hearts are firm, secure in the LORD.
Their hearts are steady, they will not be afraid;
    in the end they will look in triumph on their foes.
They have distributed freely, they have given to the poor;
    their righteousness endures forever;
    their horn is exalted in honor.
The wicked see it and are angry; they gnash their teeth and melt away;
    the desire of the wicked comes to nothing.

# Intercessions:

**Leader**: The Son of God, Lord of heaven and earth, made his home among us. With thankfulness and gladness for all the years that the N. family has lived in this home, let us call upon our God, saying: Lord, hear our prayer.
*Either individuals may be chosen for each of the petitions or one person may pray all of them.*

Taking Leave of Your Home

Person 1: Lord God, you called Abraham to leave his home and to go to a new place that you would show him. Be with this family as the members leave their home and travel to a new one. We pray to you, Lord.

**All**: Lord, hear our prayer.

**Person 2**: Lord God, through your servant, Moses, you led your chosen people out of slavery to freedom in the promised land. Lead this family to the freedom the members will enjoy in their new home. We pray to you, Lord.

**All**: Lord, hear our prayer.

**Person 3**: Lord God, you protected your people with a pillar of cloud by day and a pillar of fire by night. Protect this family from all danger as the members move into their new home. We pray to you, Lord.

**All**: Lord, hear our prayer.

**Person 4**: Lord God, you strengthened your prophet Elijah with food for his journey to your holy mountain. Strengthen this family with your Holy Spirit as the members move into their new home. We pray to you, Lord.

**All**: Lord, hear our prayer.

**Person 5**: Lord God, you sent your angel Raphael to accompany Tobias on his journey. May this family leave here in good health and arrive in good health in the members' new home. We pray to you, Lord.

**All**: Lord, hear our prayer.

**Person 6**: Lord God, you provided a flaming pillar of fire as a guide for your people's journey and a harmless sun for their wandering. Give good weather to this family on the members' moving day. We pray to you, Lord.

**All**: Lord, hear our prayer.

**Person 7**: Lord God, you were welcomed by Abraham and Sarah as a guest in their tent, and you have accepted the hospitality of this family. May the members receive all visitors in their new home as they would welcome you. We pray to you, Lord.

**All**: Lord, hear our prayer.

## Our Father

**Leader**: Let us bring all our prayers together in one and pray as Jesus taught us.
*All say the Lord's Prayer together.*

## Concluding Prayer

**Leader**: Lord, be close to your servants who move out of this home today. They thank you for all the blessings they have received here even as they ask your blessing on their move to a new home. Shelter them when they are at home, accompany them when they are away, and welcome them when they return. When they have no need of an earthly home, receive them into your world where you live for ever and ever.

**All**: Amen.

## Dismissal

**Leader**: Let us take our leave of this home in the peace of Christ.

**All**: Thanks be to God.

www.ingramcontent.com/pod-product-compliance
Lightning Source LLC
LaVergne TN
LVHW021624080426
835510LV00019B/2752